AMERICAN QUEERS

POEMS

JESSE MAVRO DIAMOND

Červená Barva Press
Somerville, Massachusetts

I0223882

Copyright © 2023 by Jesse Mavro Diamond

All rights reserved. No part of this book may be reproduced in any manner without written consent except for the quotation of short passages used inside of an article, criticism, or review.

Červená Barva Press
P.O. Box 440357
W. Somerville, MA 02144-3222

www.cervenabarvapress.com

Bookstore: www.thelostbookshelf.com

Cover Art: Ann O'Connell

Cover Design: Ann O'Connell

ISBN: 978-1-950063-77-2

Library of Congress Control Number: 2023939556

ACKNOWLEDGMENTS

PREVIOUS PUBLICATIONS WITH THANKS:

"Watch your berries, Boys," Clyde Wendell Smith, The Real Paper, 1972 ; "Fragments," Sojourner, 1981 & Mediterranean Poetry: an odyssey through the Mediterranean world (on-line) 2023; "To Princess Claude Wherever She Is Dancing," The Boston Collection Of Women's Poetry, 1983; "We Are The People," On The Purple Circuit, `1996; "Ode to a Lute," Lesbian Review of Books, 2001 & The Galway Review, 2020 & Mediterranean Poetry: an odyssey through the Mediterranean world (on-line), 2023; "Sip-In:1966," Writers Resist., 2021; "Simple Acts,"& "The Uglies," The Galway Review, 2022.

TABLE OF CONTENTS

Those Who Came After

Notes

Discussion Topics

To those who came before: *Ikh tseyln meyn brakas.*
(*I count my blessings.*)

To those who come after: *Tseyln deyn brakas.*
(*Count your blessings.*)

For Charley Shively

And Always, For Annie

Our guilt ruins our pleasure. Our guilt abuses our love...Simply sharing our bodies makes us feel Queer, outcast, unwanted; makes us despise ourselves, despise those like us and in the past has made us run after our oppressors for love, approval, support and justification. What must be eliminated is not our behavior— it needs to be savored and multiplied— but our inside feeling of wrongness.

Charley Shively, *Fag Rag*, 1972

FORWARD

I am not only a casualty; I am also a warrior.

Audre Lourde, *The Transformation of Silence into Language and Action* (1978)

When I stood on the side of the road in New Paltz, New York, 1969, watching the parade of my peers pass on their way to Woodstock, I did not join them. I knew, without question, I did not belong. I did not belong because although I shared my generation's belief that we were all androgynous, I was beyond androgyny: I was homosexual. From the earliest moments of my preadolescent life, I became increasingly aware there was something terribly wrong with my sexual desires. The love I experienced was not embraced by the Love Generation. The girls who haunted my dreams were cotton candy: they always disappeared with the first touch of my tongue.

During the 1960's and 1970's in the United States, this ignominious reality was clearly evident. Through the image of a car's locked trunk, the poem "Drive-In, c. 1966" speaks of that locked closet in which we were imprisoned. Although the characters' names and situations are imagined, the reality of living a hidden, subterranean life most certainly is not.

Stephen Gordon, the lesbian protagonist of Radcliffe Hall's 1928 seminal novel *The Well of Loneliness*, was therein labeled an invert. She heart wrenchingly delivers this final line, God…Give us also the right to our existence! Reading that line at age fifteen, in 1964, I identified with Stephen: her secret was my secret. The passage of almost a century reveals Stephen's plea has been granted to many, but not to all. In 2021, according to The Trevor Project's National Survey on LGBTQ Youth Mental Health,

Two in 5 LGBTQ youth in the United States have seriously considered suicide in the past year, a sobering survey…showing what one expert called 'the devastating mental health consequences of society's failure to create a safer and more affirming environment for America's queer youth.'

My generation's achievement of gay civil rights hailed our victory standing upon the shoulders of Hall and all the other Stephens. Today's LGBTQI community continues the battle, blowing their bugle's cry for gender fluidity upon the shoulders of the Mid-Century Queer Movement's activists.

These poems salute four leaders of that movement: Charley Shively, Stormé DeLarverie, Richard Leitsch, and Pat Parker. Although no longer alive to hear our contemporary queer youth acknowledge them for their remarkable courage, if I have been successful infusing these lines with the rhythm of teach one's inspirational breathing, readers may once again hear the beating of these full, red American hearts.

LGBTQI: The L stands for Lesbian; the G stands for Gay; the B stands for bisexual; the T stands for Trans; & the I stands for Intersex

Kingdom Of Queer

King: Stormé DeLarverie
December 24, 1920-May 24, 2014

Stone wall

(n.)A structure of stone
built up to enclose, divide,
support or protect.

Usage:

1. Take a polaroid of that gorgeous queen in front
of the crumbling stone wall.

2. Rip a brick from that
crumbling stone wall and
use it to defend yourself.

3. Old Stone Wall...tumbling down
tumbling...tumbling down
Old... Wall...

Pariahs' Paradise: 1966

The Genovese crime family bought the dump:
51 and 53 Christopher Street, New York, NY.
A peephole in the door, no liquor license,
weekly payoffs to the cops, no fire exits,
no running water at the bar, reused glasses
rinsed in a tub of water, overflowing toilets.
No Lily Law, Alice Blue Gown, Betty Badge allowed.

In a city of almost 8 million,
the only bar where gay men could dance.
It was one of the most diverse places in The City:
Whites, Blacks, Hispanics, teenagers, seventy somethings,
drag queens, closeted fags and closeted dykes
drinking from filthy glasses, pissing in shitty toilets.

Was it worth it?
What do you think?

Lily Law, Alice Blue Gown, Betty Badge were terms for
undercover police.

The Night King Storm's Lineage Was Proven

Christmas Eve, 1920.
Father: white, wealthy.
Mother: Black, poor.
Child: Black, poor.
Repeatedly attacked, scarred from
The Uglies hanging her on a fence.

Fast Forward:
At 15 she started hitting back.
That's how champions are born.

One year later, June 1936.
The night is hot as hell. Joe Lewis v. Max Schmeling.
In the twelfth round, Schmeling, Hitler's man, knocks out Joe's
lights.
The sound of The Brown Bomber hitting the floor
is the roar of Hope crashing to its knees.

Fast forward thirty-three years:
This night, as well, was hot as hell,
when the NY cops went to gather gays
like cattle into the vans.

June 28, 1969:
Seymour Pine was used to rounding up queers.
But this night the queers locked cops inside
with the sword they pulled from stone:
an uprooted parking meter.

As one dyke was dragged into the police van,
the Army of Lovers heard her shout,

WHY DON'T YOU DO SOMETHING?!

Stormé did.

The King Crowns The Cop

Line up, all you queers, queens,
dagger dykes, and city dregs.
We 're about to bust your balls!
Whether you have 'em or not. Ha! Ha! Ha!

She looked
20.
She was
48.
Don't touch me!
Some fool cop
hit her.
She hit back.
She walked away
with a bloody eye.
He didn't walk at all.
He was down, out:
busted.

The Uglies

Stormé called them the Uglies:
the bulldog ignorant bastards
who shouted, spat at, threw stones, tripped up,
kidnapped, raped and beat ordinary loving folk.

There were cliques of the Uglies, gangs of the Uglies,
ugly politicians who pandered to the Uglies,
especially at election time.
Oh yes, especially then.

Stormé had two royal superpowers.

One:
She could detect Uglies from miles away,
in the darkest streets of Greenwich Village,
during a blinding rainstorm.

And because:
she would never have let the Uglies attack
her loving girls without a damn good fight,

Two:
The ability against all the odds
to be victorious in the end.

Black and Blue

The womb she emerged from was an androgynous crucible.
When she sprang fully grown from the Jewel Box,
all previous identities melded into the King.
Each identity, white, black, girl, boy, woman, man,
was contiguous, as a rainbow.
And my oh my, she was one hot crooner.
Go ahead, compare her to
Perry, Bing, Frank.
You'll see.

What you won't see
is the wallet photo in the pocket
of those tuxedo pants.

Just once, there was love.

Since I Fell for You

Stormé's crooning,
eyes closed

> *You ooo made me leave my happy ho o ome*
> *You took my love and now you're gone*

    hot!

        Diana   dancing

                        slowly

    around

                    around
        around

   Hotter!

> *Now I'll never see the light*
> *I get the blues most every night*

   Boiling!

opening those regal eyes
looking   looking—

   Gone!

King Storm Defeats The Fearsome Uglies

The nation had long been conquered by the Uglies.
An entire country waits, year after year, starving for
America The Beautifuls to begin their resistance.

In Washington, Congress, the Supreme Court,
in This Land is Your Land, This Land is My Land,
planted in the fields of corn growing high as an elephant's eye,
in the seeds sewn by Johnny You Know Who
and the apples plucked and baked in the apple pies,
the Uglies have infected the population's majority
 with a virus that clouded the head first, then hardened the heart,
then spasmodically curled and closed the hands
in locked fists.

No longer.

King Storm confronted face to face
a band of Uglies dressed in their typical martial uniforms:
nightsticks, guns, brass knuckles, foul language and authority.
Single handedly, with fingers like vice grips,
she grabbed one Ugly so tight,
his red, white and blue blooded pulse
was completely cut off, causing him to collapse.

Within minutes,
the historically silenced, bullied Beauties
sprang into action, punching, kicking, brawling,
and screaming their echoing cry,
We're Here!   He're Here!
We're Queer!   We're Queer!
Get used to it!   Get used to it!   Get used to it!

Queen: Dick Leitsch
May 11, 1935-June 22, 2018

Sip-In: 1966

Carpenters, bankers, bricklayers, undertakers.
Why gay bars?
Because we could only be gay
In gay bars.

The N.Y. State Liquor Authority CEO:
No discrimination in bars. Why?
Because bars had the right to refuse customers
not acting suitably. Therefore, disorderly.

Bankers, bricklayers, undertakers, carpenters.
And Dick, a former Tiffany salesman.
All risking entrapment.
Wasn't flirtation with a cute, undercover cop
worth the risk?

At the West Village bar.
John, Richard, Craig and Randy
dropped the "H" word bomb.
We are homosexuals and we want a drink.
Craig, Randy, John and Richard,
I can't serve you!
You're not suitable! Therefore disorderly!

It's true:
When a carpenter has sex with a banker
or a bricklayer has sex with an undertaker
or a John has sex with a Craig
or a Randy has sex with a Richard

Being orderly is simply not suitable.

Four Deviates, One Poet

Never plan alone.
It's not Rosa Park. It's Parks.
It's not civil right. It's rights.

Thus, the group:
Myself, Craig, John, Randy.
And…ta da! The photographer.

Now, our haiku:

We are homosexuals.
We are orderly.
We are asking for service.

And the predictable, suitable bartender,
takes his hand out of his pocket
places it over the mouth of the glass, and says,

I can't serve you.

Then, the photographer
armed with a Nikon f 35 mm aims and shoots
Click click! Click click! Click!

Home for a few drinks.
Off to bed. Wake up
to a cup of freeze-dried coffee.

Open The Voice.
There it is! The evidential beauty of it all:
Four Deviates Invite Exclusion By Bar.

Mmm…Good to the last drop.

Triptych
The Unfortunates/ Found Poem #1

Well-behaved homosexuals cannot be barred from a drink...
In our culture, homosexuals are indeed unfortunates...
But their status does not make them criminals or outlaws.
excerpt The New Jersey Supreme Court, 1967

Well behaved homosexuals cannot be barred from misfortune...
In our culture, homosexuals cannot be barred from criminals ...
our status does not bar us from outlaws...

homosexuals are indeed unfortunates...
But our status does bar us from a drink.

The Unfortunates/Found Poem #2

 Among the commissioner's early regulations adopted in 1934… no licensee shall allow in the licensed premises **"any known criminals, gangsters, racketeers, pick-pockets, swindlers, confidence men, prostitutes, female impersonators, or other persons of ill repute**… *In 1950 revised to include an express prohibition of 'foul, filthy, indecent or obscene language or conduct."*

   excerpt, The New Jersey Supreme Court, 1967

 Among early regulations no licensee shall allow in the licensed premises any known criminals, **(other than the Bonano Family***),* *gangsters* **(other than the Columbo Family***),* *racketeers,* **(other than the Gambino Family)***, swindlers,* **(other than the Genovese Family),** *persons of ill repute* **(other than the Lucchese Family)**… *revised in 1950 to include an express prohibition of foul, filthy, indecent or obscene language or conduct spoken by prostitutes, female impersonators, fags or dykes.*

The Unfortunates/Found Poem #3

Miss Pucci unfortunate?
Miss Pucci Revlon
Made herself a fortunate queen
At Murphy's Tavern in Newark.

And in the ballrooms.
My oh my, she was not shy
To strut her criminal booty!

Muse: Pat Parker
June 20, 1944-June 17, 1989

Where will you be when they come?

And they will come—
They will come...because we are defined as opposite...perverse
And we are perverse.

Where Will You Be, Pat Parker, 1978

beginnings

Black in Texas,
dirt poor in a tin house,

by God, the girl was bound
for nowhere and nothing

Unless...

by the skin of her teeth
she persevered, poking through the detritus
of human waste lands hewn with hatred,
fertilized with fear

And then...

through savage determination she searched,
beneath her scorched feet, spotted Pan's pipes
lifted them boldly to her parched lips
And blew the blues away, all the way

To The Promised Land:
Oakland, Berkeley and the East Bay.

Lines

1

my lines
to your lines

are white to   black
middle class to   poverty
single woman to   married woman
step mother to   birth mother
one never raped to   one raped repeatedly
one never beaten to   one beaten repeatedly

but...

both
my lines & your lines
are not invited to
family weddings

2
your lines

are the
rope the
body the
naked
hanging man
your lines
are the
rope the
head the
neck the
bosom the
naked hanging
woman
the bound hands
the bound feet
the parched tongues
hanging

o my sister
your lines are
the omitted
lines

3
call and response lines

I hear
the wind humming
through redwoods
as you lay dying
upon a high branch
black bird calling
her sundown song

> *I am the Black woman & I have been all over**

through scrub pines
as I live singing
red bird calling
her sunrise song

> *You are the Black woman &You have been all over**

I hear you calling

> *In my dream*
> *i can walk the streets*
> *holding hands with my lover***

I hear myself responding

> *In my dream*
> *i can walk the streets*
> *holding hands with my lover***

I imagine
your gone breast
whispering in the locker room

Take away the towel
i am the scar of a wounded warrior
and I have been everywhere***

the locker room walls
echoing

you are the scar of a wounded warrior
and you have been everywhere***

You are the flower
these lines are the bee
your pollen
sticks to these lines
these lines will carry your pollen
everywhereeverywhereeverywhere

Look!

there is a woman
sitting in the June grass
reading your sticky lines

Suddenly!

a line flies off the page

dissembles to letters

starts buzzing

Past tense, present tense, future tense

your gone body carried you
your memoried body carries you
your forewings will carry you

to that woman who is a flower
petals open, waiting
for the honey of your pointed tongue

*Pat Parker's line from "Movement In Black"

** Pat Parker's lines from "I have a dream"
*** see Sister Love: The Letters of Audre Lorde and Pat Parker
1974-1989

Court Jester: Charley Shively
December 8, 1937-October 6, 2017

Charley's Ghost Visits with Walt in Hand

I am strolling on a Cambridge street in June,
as an electric blue 1966 Chevrolet Impala convertible pulls over.
Its top is down, but the windows are up.

One of the men inside whistles as I pass.
I turn to give him a piece of my mind —
LOL! It's Charley driving, The Bearded One at his side,

In his cocked, wide brimmed, felt hat.
Charley!
I can't hear you, he says, *rolling down the window.*

Looking at The Bearded One I ask,
Are you who I think you are?
I can't hear you, he says, *rolling down his window.*

Charley, the Ghost of Gay Liberation Past, adds,
We the people weren't whistling at you.
We were whistling at something we just set free.

Never mind that, I say,
Sensing he's moving toward
His lascivious poetics.

Listen, since both of you are gone,
But both of you are here,
What are you doing?

I am about to celebrate the body electric, says You Know Who.
And I will follow by shockingly pronouncing as many crude words as possible,
Charley adds.
He begins unbuttoning The Beard's linen shirt.

The Beard unbuckles Charley's bib overalls.
Bye, Guys, I say quickly,
Since I really don't want to stick around

For the celebration of their electric selves
And the shocking words to come.
It begins to rain.

They roll up their windows.
Charley turns on the car, puts it in reverse, peels back,
Jumps the curb, hits a metal garbage can

Sending it tumbling and turning in the road.
So much for state mandated garbage!
Charley the Anarchist shouts.

Putting the pedal to the metal,
They rip into the horizon
At the speed of memory.

I won't forget you, Charley! I shout.
Setting right the garbage can,
I begin again

Strolling and whistling,
Following their burnt rubber tracks
Down the vanishing road.

Simple Acts

We constantly are driven to search for simple acts of love and kindness.

Charley Shively, *Fag Rag*, 1972

Our guilt abuses the love we share.
Charged with crimes, we are innocent.
Freedom from reproach is so scarce, so rare.

Our love is a rabbit scurrying here and there,
Camouflaged by undergrowth, breathless, spent.
Our shame abuses the love we share.

The ladder to Heaven: this lover's body, bare.
With kisses, scale the leg, the torso's firmament.
Simple acts of loving are so scarce, so rare.

The antidote to toxic fear?
Break the fast of self-imposed Lent.
Take your tongue, another's blessed breast, bare.

To each, to all, raise this simple cup of care.
Exonerate ourselves; we are innocent!
Simple acts of redemption are so scarce, so rare.

This song is your roughhewn bed, simple, spare.
Fill it with two torsos, two tongues, two breasts bare.
Raise the resurrection flag, until, so sweetly spent,
We savor, we sanctify the love we share.

Those Who Came After

Drive-In, c. 1967

Betty said she didn't mind.
Robby said, *Jump in, Babe.*
He shut the trunk door with her laughter.
We paid $1.50 less.
But Betty had the trunk key in her jeans' pocket.
I could see the screen: it was blank.
Robby's girl's face was blank.

Robby and his girl Eddy made out pretty good.
I sat alone next to Betty's blank seat,
locked inside with her laughter.

Betty went home.
Her house was dark
except for her father's laughter.
He sat alone on his La-Z-Boy,
in front of the T.V.
The screen was blank.
Her mother's chair was blank.
She hid behind her locked door.

I went home,
dreaming of being tucked inside
Betty's back pocket.

When I came out, I wanted Betty.
But it was Sue Ellen who drove me to the bar
with her friend Karen in the back seat
whom Sue Ellen said, *I got right here,*
tapping her back pocket.
K's into junk, she said.

Karen went into the bathroom.
She locked herself in.
She came out.
Her face was blank
as she danced alone to the music.

Sue Ellen drew me close, laughing,
Karen won't mind, Jump in, Babe.
But even then, it was Betty.
It was always Betty.
My arms were full.
Sue Ellen's arms were full.
Karen's arms were full.

And when Betty's father needed a laugh,
he pointed his gun at her mother's door
and shot it full of blanks.

To Princess Claude, Wherever She Is Dancing

A long time ago,
before I met the woman, whose face became
 the queen in the hand I dealt myself,
there was a woman without a name.

I found her dancing in the back-street bar
that was our home, shaking her arms,
blessing each sorrowed joint,
keening it out.

That night she lay on a mattress
in the middle of my living room,
telling me, *You belong on a Harley,*
dressed in silver studs and black leather.

She wanted me tough for her.
She wanted me to protect her.
I called this woman Claude.
Claude, whom I found months later

In a medieval ward where Thorazine was King.
Some spent their whole lives there,
shuffling homage through shadowy halls.
Claude, whom I met once again,

In another ward, her eyebrows shaven,
wearing long sleeves to cover the tiny holes in her arms.
What happens to a woman like Claude?
Shuffled from partner to partner--

Always discarded
never harbored,
like a queen
in the hand?

"Watch your berries, Boys,

It's the fruit fly season," cautions the man at Joe's Place.
Watch your woman, too, you can never tell
Who will be after her, now can you?
Buddy Guy is just another guy,
Yet his blue song rips my belly apart
Like Percy's did, good old Percy,
The man who really knows what it's like
To love a woman.

Well so do I, Boys,
So do we, all 52% of us, this majority
That's been buried under your berries
For too many tunes. So watch 'em, Boys,
Because we are: the fruit fly not worth a warning,
This red heart forgotten in the blue man's song.

Anecdotes

that
butch
telling this butch
behind an ivy league building
When my woman
Doesn't do what I say
I slap her upside the head

the
sign
in the
gay bar
Prov, R. I.
1973
You're here
to drink
Not think

that
woman's legs
on top
of this
woman
a one
night stand
repeatedly
poking
poking
poking
a finger
inside
saying
I want to be
I want to be
I want to be
a man for
you, baby!

the
dawn,
walking
passing
a man
the
man's hand
grabbing
this woman's
breast
saying,
Good morning!

the
two dozen roses
her lover
sent
June 2004
Camb, Mass.
the high school office
principal
admiring
reading the card
realizing

one woman loves another woman!

she
turns away
goes into
her office
slams
the door

the
students discovering
their teacher is
Gay!

giggling, asking
What sort
of woman
is your
type?

the
school discipline officer
in the elevator
after the doors close
laughs
tells her
It's so funny
I keep
assuring my mother
I'm not gay.
I'm not gay.
I'm not gay.

i put my love away

in my pocket
a switchblade
ready to strike

i put my love away
each day
as i set off for work
where there's a woman
who thinks
the YWCA is weird
because there are dykes around
but she won't say the word
she won't say why
she puts that word away
like the feminine thing she is
like a metal file in her shoe

i put my love away
a switchblade
closed
but ready to strike
ready to strike
at the poor man
who's just been had
by some rich man
he licks his teeth
his lips are the switch
his tongue the blade
he clicks open

Faggot! he swipes
Faggot! he swipes again
and again *Faggot!*

i make no cry
when he cuts
because
i've put my words

away
i hate that woman
i hate that man
we all hate each other

in the end
one thing is
worse
than putting our
love away:
taking it out
honed from
each harassment
harassed
a hundred times

we are poisoned
we are snakes,
coiling
rattling

ready to strike!

Fragments

Sappho, it was long, long ago that I
like Leda, saw wild hyacinths--
and found beneath them
an egg.

But the firecracker flower is a frozen bulb
in the winter. The budding flame
that ran under my skin, has burst,
is buried.

Still, I keep this lavender ribbon.
I am dark, like you, and have known the one
with blue eyes-- it was then I sang
your song.

And now--I cut this brown hair,
my curls scatter with the chestnuts in her yard.
I watch the apple branches admonish me
in a cold wind.

When the leaves fall and the daylight lessens,
my heart will drop like a red fruit—
She is leaving me: her pointed lips,
her pink blossom.

Motorcycle Momma

I love a motorcycle momma,
She picks me up and lays me down again.
I love a motorcycle momma,
She picks me up and lays me down again.
She asks me to come outside and play with her,
There's no good reason to stay in.

She's got her brown leather jacket, Girls,
Got her brown sunset eyes and soft brown skin.
She's got her brown leather jacket, Boys,
Got her brown sunset eyes and soft brown skin.
When that old sun starts slipping down inside
Her eyes weep for night, I have a real good friend.

When we're cruising down Main Street,
Everybody bound to turn around and stare.
Cruising down Main Street,
Everybody bound to turn around and stare.
Flashing their looks just like stop lights,
Keep on flashing 'cause me and my momma
We don't care.

I'll tell you why:

I love a motorcycle momma,
She picks me up and she lays me down again.
I love a motorcycle momma,
She picks me up and lays me down again.
Well, she asks me to come outside and play with her.
There's no good reason to stay in.

We The People: 1973

We the people are strolling along the river.
We stroll along the river one by one and two by two.
We the people are strolling along the river.
We are the common people.
We are the common people without common sense,
Without sense enough to live in a decent fashion,
Without decency enough to fashion our lives after others.
We are the courageous people.

We are the ones who live so courageously we are afraid.
Courage is not a virtue in this world.
Courage does not bring us jobs.
Courage does not rent us apartments.
Courage does not rule favorably in the courts.
Courage does not look good.

Courage is our undoing, they will be sure of that.
They will make certain we won 't live in peace.
They will make certain we are miserable in our happiness.
They will fire us and evict us as they always have.
They will rape our women and beat our men.
They will not be charged for their crimes against us.

They will call our love for each other unnatural.
They will prove scientifically it cannot be so,
as they always, always have.

When we are dead they will praise us,
Just as they now praise Sappho and Oscar Wilde,
Gertrude Stein and Baudelaire,
Just as they praise their own daughters and sons,
Carol and John, sons and daughters, David and Karen,
Who disgraced them when they lived
Whom they praise now that their children
Are no longer alive to hear them,
Now that they are no longer alive to revolt them.

Yes, we are the people who revolt them:

We are the tough women and the gentle men,
We are the gentle women and the tough men,
We are the bald-headed girls in leather,
We are the long-haired boys in lavender,
We are the long-haired women and the shaven men,
We re mothers, we are fathers, we are sisters, we are brothers.
We are the common people.

We are the people who stroll along the river.
We are strolling one by one and two by two.
We are walking by the hundreds,
By the thousands we are marching together,
Hundreds of thousands singing together,
Millions shouting our desire in their ears.

We will go on screaming
Until they recognize our cry,
Until they finally understand
We need our lovers to go on living just as they do.

They can bully us in Boston.
They can burn us in New Orleans.
They can beat us in San Francisco.
They can bury us in Queens.

But they cannot deny us our desire
Which is our hunger.
They cannot deny us our love
Which is our bread.

Listen well for we are the people
And we are screaming.

Princes of Pulse

Luis Daniel Wilson Leon
February 26, 1979-June 12, 2016

Remember when I told you what it was like in P.R.?
*Pequeña cuidad, pequeñas mentes**
You said, But this is Florida!
Land of the free! For you I choose Declaration by Cartier,
Because you have declared your freedom!
Carlito, now it is my turn to sell this to you.
Imagine: a child, a family,
A rich life is the most intense perfume.
Don't close your eyes,
Be brave, say Si.
Say after me, Si, Si claro.
Come closer.
I can't hear you.
Whisper your declaration in my ear.

Jean Carlos Mendez Perez
July 27, 1980 – June 12, 2016

We were holding hands, discussing children;
A child, you asked, *should we have one ?*
Why not? You'd make a great dad.
But I shook my head,
let go of your hand,
closed my eyes, finally said,
I don't know, I don't know.
Oh, Mi Principe,
I smell the rain falling on our grassy bed.
Mi Amor, let me say instead,
I never meant I loved you less.
Yes, yes.
Let's,
Yes.

**little city, little minds*

Ode To A Lute

Spring

In April, at the bottom of the stairs, we found a stringless lute.
I saw it first, you claimed. Besides, you joked, you're Sephardic,
a horse thief, whereas I, Russian, Ashkenazi, am no criminal.
Take the lute, I said, and take this story, too.
If a person steals a horse, she may be on the run
from worse thieves, chasing her out
of her own country. Imagine, she has no alternative
but to grab the first horse she sees, jump on it
and gallop hundreds of miles into a strange land,
changing her name as she rides, covering her face with a rag,
even at night, so the moonlight will not reveal
her true identity. Understand? I asked.
But you had fallen asleep in my lap, cradling the lute.

Summer

I dream I am on a commuter train, stopped between stations.
I am strumming the lute when I look into the next car
and see you reading poetry. Your hair is red, curly
as when you were eighteen. Rising, I move through the door
which separates us. I sit down next to you and
we begin laughing. Leaning over, I kiss your cheek,
handing you the lute. I speak to you in Yiddish, saying,
This dream is the song my heart sings. But weeping, you say,
I live far away, there are children now. The doors open,
you rise, leaving me sitting in this car filled with strangers.
The doors close, the wheels begin turning, the train moves
forward, back to this empty bed where the July dawn
raises its humid curtain on this open-air theater
and the southern wind hisses at me through green lips.

Autumn

Mercury found a hollow tortoise shell tossed upon the beach.
Its origin, like ours, was Egypt. Although the turtle's flesh was
eroded, its nerves remained; despite an echoing moan
in the animal's soul, when the god strummed those nerves,
the cords sprang to life, and his fingers became falcon's wings.
Apollo's story insists he invented the blessed bowl,
fashioning it from his sister's bow, whose strings
sang as her arrow flew. He must have stolen the bow.
I won't be persuaded she gave it up. Perhaps they wrestled
for the prize, as I once did for you. Why must it always be gods
who make the sweetest music, their lyrics lancing a woman's heart?
Mercury, god of casual love, Apollo, merely handsome.
But I, a plain woman, a rabbit, spend loveless nights running
from the moon's skinning knife through dry September grasses.

Winter

As you lay sleeping, curved against my breast,
inlaid mother of pearl circled its open mouth.
It was December, yet the birds flew in and out of the blithe wood
and the Hudson sang unfrozen between its banks.
We travelled as far as the lute, from the Nile to the Aegean,
to the Adriatic, to Venice, Rome, Paris and Vienna,
this diaspora of song, with verses belonging to one poem.
I await you here, by the riverside where we parted.
The *shmatte* which covers my face is this poem.
On my back I carry a hollow tortoise shell.
I pray you will find me, cradle me, claim me as your own.
Time has eroded my flesh, but my nerves remain.
I long to sit next to you, to hear you whisper my name.
Come, *Liebling*, sing to me, bring me to our home.

Shmatte, (Yiddish) rag
Liebling, (Yiddish) Darling

NOTES

Inscription: For Charley

Charley Shively

Shivley's seminal research on Walt Whitman resulted in two books—*Calamus Lovers: Walt Whitman's Working Class Camerados* (1987) and *Drum Beats: Walt Whitman's Civil War Boy Lovers* (1989)—

According to Jim Downs (*Outward*, October 12, 2017) Charley was:

"A pioneering gay liberation activist…journalist, poet, founding editor of one of the most important gay newspapers in the 1970's (*Fag Rag*)…Shively and many others of his generation fundamentally rejected the pillars of American society—religion, capitalism, and the family. The popular political 1970s liberation slogan sums it up best: 'Two, four, six, eight, smash the church, smash the state…' Shively spent his career writing about how gay people understood their bodies, relationships, and sex. For him, writing about sex was political; he once wrote a series on oral sex as a revolutionary act, addressing the unacknowledged guilt and shame many gay men faced engaging in it. … Shively interrogated the sex that propelled (gay men) to become political in the first place. He shed light on the taboos that many gay men were too uneasy to discuss in public: the mechanics of sex, intimacy between men, the question of promiscuity… At the Boston gay pride march on June 18, 1977, (see below), Shively stood on stage in his academic regalia—which he earned from his Ph.D.at Harvard University. He told the crowd that his request for teaching gay history at Boston State College was denied. He then said his Harvard diploma was useless, so he lit it on fire. The crowd roared…*He was one of the most brilliant minds of the last century, and we all need to know his name.*"

Excerpt from "Boston Bible Burning Transcript of Charley Shively's keynote address at Boston's Gay Pride Rally, June 18, 1977." (from *Fag Rag* 20 Summer 1977.

I have a Harvard PhD. and I teach at Boston
State College: they say I'm not fit to teach
Gay History:
I have here the committee report calling me
unqualified.
I have here my Harvard diploma.
They are worth only burning.
(*cheers for the burning papers*)
In today's march, we passed by the John
Hancock Insurance and the Prudential Insurance
buildings; these companies have one
hundred, two hundred, a thousand times
more space than all the gay bars and all the
gay organizations in Boston.
I have here an insurance policy and a dollar
bill.
This is what they're worth: Burning.
(*cheers at the flames*)
I have here the text of the crimes against
chastity, Chapter 272, Verse 32 of the Massachusetts
Criminal Code:
"Whoever commits the abominable and detestable
crime against nature, either with
mankind or with a beast, shall be punished
by imprisonment in the state prison for not
more than twenty years."
The laws of the state against us are only
worth burning.
(*cheers and shouts of Burn it! Burn it!*)
I have here the Bible. Leviticus, Chapter 20
says: "If a man also like (lie) with mankind, as he
lieth with a woman, both of them have committed
an abomination: they shall surely be
put to death; their blood shall be upon them."
And "A man also or woman that hath a familiar
spirit, ...shall surely be
put to death: they shall stone them with
stones: their blood shall be upon them."
(*cheers and shouts of 'Burn it! Burn it!'*
Combined with, *No, no, not the Bible; You can't burn the Bible*

after the Bible drops into the flames and ignites, an excited demonstrator grabs and stamps on it with his feet.)
Nine million witches have been burnt to death under that verse.
And how many gay people we will never know, but the word
'faggot' comes from tying us to the feet of the nine million witches
as they burned to
death, which is what it means to say 'burn a
faggot.'
So, when Anita Bryant quotes those
verses, she's talking about our MURDER!
WE CANNOT COMPROMISE;
WE CANNOT SINK INTO RESPECTABILITY.
Some among us may think you don't have to
worry...
But when the time comes, we are not going to be asked
what degrees we have,
how rich we are, who we know or what we
have accomplished. They will only ask, 'Are
you queer?' and when they come for the
queers, they are going to come for us all.
WE MUST COME TOGETHER OR WE WILL
SURELY BE DESTROYED.

See also, "In Memoriam: Charley Shively, 1937-2017," Ed Folsom, *Walt Whitman Quarterly Review*, Volume 35, Number 2, 2017

King: Stormé DeLarverie

Poems connected to this information include "Stone wall"; " The Night King Storm's Lineage Was Proven"; 'The Uglies"; 'King Storm Defeats The Fearsome Uglies."

This excerpt from her obituary, by William Yardley, May 29, 2014, The New York Times, captures the essential role DeLarverie played in The Mid-Century Movement:

"… was indisputably one of the first and most assertive members of the modern gay rights movement…

No one questions whether Ms. DeLarverie was there on June 27, 1969, the night the police raided the Stonewall Inn, a gay bar, setting off protests that helped start the gay rights movement. But was she the cross-dressing lesbian whose clubbing by the police helped set the chaos in motion? Some witnesses have said yes, others no. 'Nobody knows who threw the first punch, but it's rumored that she did, …said Ms. Cannistraci, an owner of the Village lesbian bar Henrietta Hudson. 'She told me she did.'

Ms. DeLarverie had grown up in the South, of mixed race, and spent part of the first half of her life singing and performing as a man. Identity, for her, had been especially complicated, and she did not want others persecuted for theirs. Into her 80s, patrolling the sidewalks and checking in at lesbian bars, she was on the lookout for what she called 'ugliness': any form of intolerance, bullying or abuse of her 'baby girls.'

'I can spot ugly in a minute,' she said in a 2009 interview for Columbia University's NYC in Focus Journalism Project. 'No people even pull it around me that know me. They'll just walk away, and that's a good thing to do because I'll either pick up the phone or I'll nail you.'

Queen: Dick Leitsch

In Mr. Leitsch's obituary (Dick Leitsch, whose 'Sip-In Was A Gay Rights Milestone') Robert D. McFadden describes him:

"A bartender, freelance journalist and onetime Tiffany sales representative, Mr. Leitsch was a self-described 'hick from Kentucky who didn't know anything about gay rights' when he followed a boyfriend to New York in 1959. He soon became a member and young leader of the Mattachine Society, an early gay advocacy group named after a group of medieval jesters who, disguised by masks, protested the oppression of peasants. Mr. Leitsch rarely donned a mask himself. After being named president of the organization's New York chapter in 1965, he took the group in a more aggressive direction, taking on the city's police chief and newly elected liberal mayor, John V. Lindsay, in campaigns that drew on the tactics of the African American civil rights movement and became a model for other gay rights groups across the country."

Dick Leitsch was one of the country's most militant and important gay activists in the decade before Stonewall, George Chauncey, a Columbia University historian who wrote "Gay New York" (1994), said in an email. The sip-in he organized at *Julius* is a brilliant example of lessons he took from the black civil rights movement about how to stage events that reframed public understanding. This had a profound impact on gay life in New York, Chauncey said. 'It really meant that for the first time in a generation, a gay man going into a bar didn't have to worry that the cute guy coming onto him might've been a plainclothes man who was trying to reach his arrest quota.' 'His actions,' Chauncey added, 'helped make it easier for a generation of gay people to come out and be openly gay.'

Building on the success of his anti-entrapment campaign, Mr. Leitsch organized an effort to spotlight the refusal of bars to serve gay customers, which Chauncey described as 'the first organized act of civil disobedience by gay people, following picket line protests held in cities such as New York and Philadelphia.'

Known as the Sip-In, an alcohol-infused twist on the sit-ins that African Americans held at segregated lunch counters in the South, the protest took place at the West Village bar Julius' where the

entrapment of a former Peace Corps volunteer had spurred Mr. Leitsch's police-reform effort. In a public-relations coup for Mr. Leitsch, a Village Voice photographer captured the moment on April 21, 1966, when a bartender at Julius' placed his hand over a glass, refusing service to Mr. Leitsch and his Mattachine friends Craig Rodwell, John Timmons and Randy Wicker.
According to historian David Carter's Stonewall: The Riots That Sparked the Gay Revolution,. Leitsch's Sip-In led to a growing acceptance of gays at bars in New York and across the country. Perhaps most significantly, the publicity resulted in a Mattachine lawsuit in New Jersey, where in 1967 the state Supreme Court ruled that 'well-behaved homosexuals could not be barred from a drink.'

The Unfortunates/Found Poem #2
The pbs.org American Experience site, accessed August 11, 2022 states:
"Already a strong presence in New York, members of the Mafia saw a business opportunity in catering to the otherwise shunned gay population. By the mid-1960s, the Genovese crime family controlled the majority of gay bars in Greenwich Village, a neighborhood in southern Manhattan that was quickly becoming a hub for the city's burgeoning gay community. In 1966, young Genovese family member Tony Lauria purchased the Stonewall Inn, then a low-earning 'straight' bar and restaurant. "Fat Tony," as he was known, renovated at low cost and reopened the Christopher Street club as a gay bar, controlling everything from the jukebox to the cigarettes. He bribed New York's Sixth Police Precinct with around $1,200 a month to turn a blind eye to the goings on at the establishment."

Muse: Pat Parker

In *Pat Parker: a tribute*, (Brimstone, L. Fem. Rev. (1990) 34: 4. https://doi.org/10.1057/fr.1990.2) Lyndie Brimstone describes the connection between Parker's roots and radical voice:

"A survivor of tin-roofed 'Texas hell, soul-searing poverty and small town mentality' (Parker, 1978: 141, *'Womanslaughter'*), Pat Parker was one of the first working-class poets to wave two strong womanly fingers at the literary elite and their 'academic wanderings' (Parker, 1987: 61). Judy Grahn, a 'classmate' and friend for many years, describes her as 'an outrageous poet, the kind who says things first, and means them' (Grahn, 1978: 13).

2 your lines

According to NAACP, *History of Lynching in America,*

From 1882 to 1968, 4,743 lynchings occurred in the U.S. Many historians believe the true number is underreported.

Those Who Came After

We The People

There have been positive social changes since I wrote this poem almost 50 years ago.
Certain areas of gay life have become more equitable; some have not. A reliable source for information on advances of LGBTQ rights from 2000 to 2009 is:
https://www.lgbtmap.org/file/a-decade-of-progress-on-lgbt-rights.pdf

The Princes Of Pulse
Luis Daniel Wilson Leon and Jean Carlos Mendez Perez

From Britannica.com:

Orlando shooting of 2016
By Michael Ray • Last Updated: Feb 27, 2022

(The)Orlando shooting of 2016, also called (The) **Pulse Nightclub Shooting**, (was a) <u>mass shooting</u> that took place at the Pulse nightclub in Orlando, Florida in the early morning hours of June 12, 2016, and left 49 people dead and more than 50 <u>wounded</u>. It was the deadliest mass shooting in U.S. history up to that time.

Since its opening in 2004, Orlando's Pulse dance club had established itself as one of central Florida's most vibrant centers for <u>lesbian</u>, <u>gay</u>, <u>bisexual</u>, <u>transgender</u>, and <u>queer</u> (LGBTQ) social life. On the night of the attack, the club was hosting its popular Latin Night, an event that drew from a broad <u>cross section</u> of the <u>community</u>. Just after 2:00 AM on June 12, 2016, more than 300 people were inside the club when (the shooter) opened fire near the entrance...

The poem imagines a moment before Wilson-Leon and Mendez Perez were killed, when the lovers are having a conversation about becoming parents.

Discussion Topics

1.   Which poem(s) grab you the most? Why?
2.   In Pariah's Paradise 1966, at the end of the poem, the poets asks the reader these questions:
        Was it worth it?
        What do you think?
Answer her questions.
3.   Try reading some poems aloud or, if possible, hearing them in your mind.
Is there a poem whose "volume" the poet has somehow turned up? Why do you think she's done this?

4.   The poet plays with achieving meaning through manipulation of how words are spaced on the page. Pick a poem where this manipulation adds to the meaning. Explain how.

5.   In the section "Kingdom of Queer" which of the 4 characters, if any, do you wish you could meet in person? If you could meet them, what would you want to discuss or ask?

6.   The poet believes the life of a deceased person can be extended through narrative poems devoted to that person. Do you agree? If so, which poems have succeeded in this ?

ABOUT THE AUTHOR

Jesse Mavro Diamond has been writing poetry since childhood, when at 7, she was the proud and delighted author of her first published poem, "Summer is Over". Throughout the next six decades, her writing has explored issues of deep interest to her including identity, gender politics and the diverse societal influences that shape our lives. Mavro Diamond's experiences as a Jewish woman, feminist, martial artist, and teacher of English Language Arts at both the secondary and college level has informed every aspect of her writing. She is the author of four plays and six volumes of poetry, including *Swimming the Hellespont*, whose title poem was chosen to be honored by the Tennessee Williams Literary Festival. Most recently, she developed and taught the first Creative Writing Course in Boston Latin School's 364-year History. Her work has been published and performed within the United States and internationally.

www.ingramcontent.com/pod-product-compliance
Lightning Source LLC
Chambersburg PA
CBHW031933080426
42734CB00007B/659

9 781950 063772